I0726934

Bernard Huff

Attorney at Law and Certified Mediator

A JOURNAL OF POETIC INSPIRATIONAL EXPRESSIONS AND GUIDANCE

"A must-have arrangement of Literary Expressions
and Guidance for Youth, Adults, Groups and Organizations."

WORKBOOK PRESS LLC
187 E Warm Springs Rd,
Suite B285, Las Vegas, NV 89119, USA

Website: https://workbookpress.com/
Hotline: 1-888-818-4856
Email: admin@workbookpress.com

Ordering Information:
Quantity sales. Special discounts are available on quantity purchases by corporations, associations, and others.
For details, contact the publisher at the address above.

Library of Congress Control Number:
ISBN-13:   000-0-000000-00-0 (Paperback Version)
                000-0-000000-00-0 (Digital Version)

REV. DATE: 08/31/2022

A JOURNAL OF POETIC INSPIRATIONAL

EXPRESSIONS AND GUIDANCE

" A MUST-HAVE BOOKLET WITH AN ARRANGEMENT OF
POETIC LITERARY EXPRESSIONS AND GUIDANCE FOR
YOUTH, ADULTS, GROUPS AND ORGANIZATIONS "

CONTENTS

ABOUT THE AUTHOR

BERNARD HUFF,

ATTORNEY AND MEDIATOR

Bernard Huff is currently a licensed practicing attorney and a certified mediator in Indianapolis, Indiana. He took the extensive basic and advance mediation training courses. He has many years of legal experience and expertise in various legal areas in both public and private employment. He has served on the board of directors of several nonprofit, civic and professional organizations, including the Marion County Bar Association and Indianapolis Professional Association (IPA) as a founding member and its chairman of the board for several years. He has often served as both Chairman and Coordinator of IPA's Networking and Education Task Forces for local community-wide charitable events. In 2020, he was instrumental in getting and aiding a noted utility company to produce a professional and outstanding video about IPA and its rich history of long standing.

He has taken as well as taught various leadership courses and has been involved in extensive nonprofit organizational training. For his participation and dedication, he has been recognized for his outstanding **performance in law**. He was a recipient in both 1991 and 1993 of Distinguished Awards from the Center for Leadership Development, a noted youth organization in

Indianapolis, Indiana. He was the first recipient of the Ardath Burkhart Distinguished Alumnus Award for his outstanding board leadership and community activities. The Ardath Burkhart Board Development Leadership Series was a program of the United Way of Central Indiana. He continues to be actively involved in planning major events which pertain to mentoring, education, diversity and economic empowerment.

NOTED PUBLISHED ARTICLES

SIX OF ATTORNEY BERNARD HUFF'S NOTED PUBLICATIONS ARE AS FOLLOW:

- EFFECTIVE NETWORKING: African-American Style

- TESTING AND ITS MANY LEGAL RAMIFICATIONS

- NOTED SUPREME COURT DECISIONS ON PREVALENT EEO AND LABOR LAW MATTERS

- REVERSE DISCRIMINATION: AN EROSION OF EQUAL OPPORTUNITIES

- THE UNDERUTILIZATION OF LEGAL SERVICES OF AFRICAN-AMERICAN ATTORNEYS

- CORPORATE PARTNERING

DEDICATIONS

First and foremost, I dedicate this JOURNAL OF POETIC INSPIRATIONAL EXPRESSIONS and GUIDANCE to my late, loving and classy wife, MARCHUSA A. HUFF. I miss her presence deeply. Her outstanding contributions to the Indiana University School of Nursing and her nursing services at Community Health Network in Indianapolis will be perpetuated in many memories. In composing the several compositions after her death, I thought of her frequently and her devotion to her family, her two grandchildren (ARDEN and CALEB LAWSON), her former students, her colleagues, friends and many others. These pleasant and clear thoughts helped me to become more creative. Her family members lovingly called her "NICKEY".

I also dedicate this publication to my son, JUSTIN B. HUFF. I thank you for all of the initial work you performed in getting my first five poems into a printed bound booklet. I am forever grateful for your help. Your effort was the impetus and an additional motivation for me to write more poetry and get all of my literary creations published. THANK YOU.

INTRODUCTION TO POETIC JOURNAL OF INSPIRATIONAL EXPRESSIONS AND GUIDANCE

The following literary pieces, prose and guides were composed by Bernard Huff, Attorney at Law and Certified Mediator. In addition to Attorney Huff's professional and civic involvement, he has devoted much time and effort in creating and having different persons to recite with training and eloquence, several of the following secular literary pieces. These compositions are meant to be uplifting and motivating messages for both youth and adult in various stages of their lives. Many of the youths of this current generation are engage in worthwhile endeavors to become productive future citizens. Many are trying to make it "against the odds". It is one of the author's main aim to further encourage and inspire them to move forward to achieve greater height as they strive to improve their lives. Two recent compositions include general revelations and reactions to prevalent current events and social and business engagements by African-Americans. The last composition, M-A-M-A is a maternal acronym to be readily applied by business and civic organizations and groups.

The author wants these literary creations to be read and heard by as many people as possible. Some of the pieces, except "INTROSPECTION" (for short) and "PERSONAS", require interaction from or participation by others to get the best import and effect. "REACH UP, REACH OUT. REACH BACK" has an altruistic appeal while "EXPECT THE BEST FROM YOURSELF' and "WHAT DO YOU CHOOSE TO DO WITH YOUR LIFE" are individually directed.

Four other personal literary directives are "TAKING THE NEXT STEP(S)..." with its request to go the full distance, "INTROSPECTION", "PERSONAS" and "SELF-EMPOWERMENT". "INTROSPECTION" is an honest and personal insight and revelation for anyone who wants to engage in some "soul-searching" to find out who that person is and where he/she is headed. "PERSONAS" discloses and explores the facades we employ in our interpersonal relationships and responses to situations. "SELF-EMPOWERMENT" is a didactic composition which states and explores the qualities which we need to be self-sustaining and to guide and control our lives and destinies.

During the 2020 year, there were several unforgettable events, including the pandemic outbreak of the corona virus. Also, there was the heartfelt and diverse global, national, state and local outcries for social justice and racial equality as a result of black homicides in America by policemen. The latest creation offers remedial improvements to this continuing dark revelation in America. It has the captivating title of "A UNIFIED CRY FOR EQUALITY AND REFORMATION".

The writer hopes the readers enjoy each piece. The latter four prose-like compositions cover important and current matters of racial and social equality, diversity, networking, and MAMA, a maternal acronym to be readily use as an effective operational guide. Take the complete journey.

BERNARD HUFF

YOU COULD BE: AN EDUCATIONAL LIFE CHALLENGE

("THE CHALLENGE")

DARE

Indianapolis Professional Association, Inc.
EDUCATION &
MENTORING
IP4
ONOMIC
ELOPMENT
NETWO

YOU COULD BE: AN EDUCATIONAL LIFE CHALLENGE ("THE CHALLENGE")

YOU COULD BE—

That special elementary or high school teacher, or that college professor who has the unique ability and educational skills to mold and infuse within many of the young minds you teach, a strong sense of pride, self-worth, rightness and respect for others so that they will mature into productive pieces of humanity.

YOU COULD BE THAT EDUCATOR.

YOU COULD BE—

That compassionate doctor or dedicated scientist who diligently searches for and finds a universal cure for one of the most dreaded diseases facing mankind today.

YOU COULD BE THE NEXT PIONEER IN THE FIELD OF MEDICINE.

YOU COULD BE—

That corporate head or CEO in a large profitable company who makes all of the major decisions about how that company should operate because you would be the owner.

YOU COULD BE THAT SUCCESSFUL BUSINESS PERSON.

YOU COULD BE—

That outstanding lawyer or judge who has a sharp legal mind, a deep concern for equal justice for all, and a keen insight into the main causes of racism and other inequities in this nation and the world, and by having such knowledge, insight and concern, you devote your life toward the elimination of such injustices.

YOU COULD BE THAT OUTSTANDING ATTORNEY OR NOTED LOCAL OR SUPREME COURT JUDGE.

YOU COULD BE—

That particular engineer who build that special aircraft, which would provide affordable transportation in space for people who want to travel from one planet to the next or to the moon.

YOU COULD BE THAT NEXT INTERPLANETARY SPACE PILOT.

YOU COULD BE—

That architect with an unselfish vision, who designs and create buildings and environment that would not only accommodate the homeless and their basic needs but would materially change their lives and integrate them into the mainstream.

YOU COULD BE THAT VISIONARY.

YOU COULD BE—

That successful writer, noted movie producer or director who has that special talent to accurately and vividly depict in written words or show on the screen the real, diverse, aspiring and inspiring lives of all people within this nation.

YOU COULD BE THAT NEXT SCREEN PLAY WRITER, MOVIE PRODUCER OR DIRECTOR.

YOU COULD BE—

That human spark, that magnetic and unifying force, which would give to all races and all people, to this community and to this country, a sense of unity and purpose with your deep commitment to the welfare and well-being of all of this nation's citizens.

YOU COULD BE THE NEXT RESPONSIBLE, CARING AND TRULY CONCERNED LEADER.

YOU CAN BE anything you to be if you would only continue to follow and nurture your dreams. Education, learning and good self-discipline are the basic tools you will need to cultivate your mind. In this world, as imperfect as it may be, there will always be much room to create, many areas left to explore, and there will always be a need for some of you to continue life's relay by taking the living torch from your parents, some of our leaders, educators and other and keeping it burning.

YOU CAN DO ANYTHING YOU WANT TO DO AND BE ANYTHING YOU WANT TO BE if you continue to prepare yourself for tomorrow's world. This is my challenge to each of you.

I DOUBLE DARE YOU TO MEET IT!

WE WILL BE: THE NEXT GENERATION'S AFFIRMATION

("THE AFFIRMATION")

WILL

Indianapolis Professional Association, Inc.
EDUCATION
MENTO
IPA
ECONOMIC
DEVELOPMENT

WE WILL BE: THE NEXT GENERATION'S AFFIRMATION ("THE AFFIRMATION")

WE WILL continue to pursue our main life dreams by taking advantage of all of the opportunities that are available to us, both inside and outside the classrooms and whatever life itself may offer in our life journey.

WE WILL strive to achieve our life goals through education, self-initiatives, self-discipline, good parenting and by staying focus.

WE WILL, through different ways, request help and will need to rely on this and past generations' life experiences and we hope that you as parents, educators and leaders will be there to give us the necessary guidance and assistance for us to continue to grow and mature into productive human beings.

WE WILL take some of your knowledge or advice, may be not all of it to heart, and use it wisely to help fulfill our life dreams.

WE WILL make some mistakes from time-to-time, but hopefully, none too grave as to preclude most, if not all of us, from achieving some of our main future goals.

WE WILL do the best that we can. Be considerate and patient with us.

WE WILL be the good and caring parents, the effective educators, the prepared professionals, the scrupulous business persons, the concerned citizens and the responsible leaders in tomorrow's world.

WE WILL keep and bring these promises to a realization.

WE WILL take the living torch from the past and current generations, including our parents, when it becomes our time to do so, and **WE WILL** keep the flame burning brightly.

WE WILL readily assume that responsibility and **WE WILL** do it well.

WE WILL ACCEPT the educational life challenge for the next generation.

WE WILL MEET THAT CHALLENGE! WE WILL MEET THAT CHALLENGE!

THIS IS OUR AFFIRMATION! OUR RESPONSE!

LOOK OUT TOMORROW'S WORLD! WE WILL BE PREPARED AND READY FOR YOU!

<u>REACH UP, REACH OUT, REACH BACK</u>

("The Secondary Three R's")

REACH

24

25

REACH UP, REACH OUT, REACH BACK

"THE SECONDARY THREE R'S"

REACH UP

As far as your dreams and ability will let you

in pursuit of your life goals.

You may touch a star if your aim is sturdy,

continuing and high enough. **REACH UP!**

REACH OUT

For that willing helping hand

in times of need, disappointment and despair,

but hold on to your dreams.

There will always be someone near, a friend, parent, a peer,

who could offer and give you the necessary encouragement

you will need to restore your hope,

and help you to continue on your life journey

to worthwhile achievements. **REACH OUT!**

REACH BACK

From time to time to help others

with your unique talents and skills

on your road to and after you obtain success.

For life is most fulfilling when you reach back

and make others the beneficiaries of your

success and accomplishments. **REACH BACK!**

REACH UP!

REACH OUT!

REACH BACK!

REACH UP!

REACH OUT!

REACH BACK!

"REACH UP, REACH OUT, REACH BACK"

REACH UP, REACH OUT, REACH BACK

Lighting the New Millennium with "The Secondary Three R's"

REACH

(Millennium)

REACH UP, REACH OUT, REACH BACK

LIGHTING THE NEW MILLENIUM WITH

"THE SECONDARY THREE R'S"

Listen! teens and parents too!

As each one of you let your light shines and

illuminates throughout the new millennium,

always keep in mind and practice to the fullest

the Secondary Three R's.

REACH UP! REACH OUT! REACH BACK!

REACH UP

As far as your dreams and ability will let you

in pursuit of your life goals.

You may touch a start if your aim is sturdy,

continuous and high enough. **REACH UP!**

REACH OUT

For that willing helping hand

in times of need, disappointment and despair,

but, but hold on to your dreams.

There will always be someone near, a friend, a parent, a peer,

who could offer or give the necessary encouragement

you will need to restore your hope and

help you to continue on your life journey

to worthwhile achievements. **REACH OUT!**

REACH BACK

From time to time to help others

with your unique talents and skills

on your road to and after you obtain success.

For life is most fulfilling when you reach back

and make others the beneficiaries of your

success and accomplishments. **REACH BACK!**

Starting now and continuing, throughout the new millennium.

REACH UP! REACH OUT! REACH BACK!

REACH UP! REACH OUT! REACH BACK!

REACH UP! REACH OUT! REACH BACK!

EXPECT THE BEST FROM YOURSELF AND GET IT

("A Personal Commitment")

BEST

BUTLER UNIVERSITY
INDIANAPOLIS 1855

EXPECT THE BEST FROM YOURSELF AND GET IT ("A PERSONAL COMMITMENT")
BY ATTY. BERNARD HUFF (REVISED 10/13)

In your lifelong process of self-development, give yourself high morals and self-esteem. Consider yourself one of the best and develop enough self-assurance that you can accomplish or do anything equally as well or better than anyone else. For cockiness coupled with competence is an acceptable trait under many circumstances as you know.

EXPECT THE BEST FROM YOURSELF!!

During your adolescence and adult life, think of yourself, with modesty and humility, as an excellent example for your peers and others to follow.

EXPECT THE BEST FROM YOURSELF!!

In your worthwhile endeavors, you know that steadfast commitments, diligent work and follow-through efforts are essentials elements to achieve excellence or success in whatever you do, and you resign and condition yourself to do whatever it takes.

EXPECT THE BEST FROM YOURSELF!!

In some of your personal engagements, you may perceive and evaluate your performance, your results or yourself as being "average" or "good" but you deeply feel that you could do better and will try harder the next time eventhough others may think you did your best.

EXPECT THE BEST FROM YOURSELF!!

In your personal commitments to others, you must be honest, truthful, tactful and kind in order for others to trust and think highly of you as a son or daughter, mother or father, mate, peer, friend or human being, and you will continually try to improve on these likable attributes.

EXPECT THE BEST FROM YOURSELF!!

To fulfill your various wants and needs and to strive to obtain and maintain the richness of your dreams, you are aware that you have to prepare yourself and you will.

EXPECT THE BEST FROM YOURSELF!!

In the classroom, on your job, in establishing your career and in finding your niche in life, you know that you must develop and keep high standards for yourself and you will.

EXPECT THE BEST FOR YOURSELF!!

EXPECT THE BEST IN YOUR MEANINGFUL

RELATIONSHIPS WITH OTHERS.

EXPECT THE BEST IN YOUR MAJOR LIFE EXPERIENCES.

EXPECT THE BEST IN EVERYTHING YOU DO WORTHWHILE.

EXPECT THE BEST FROM YOURSELF. OTHERS WILL SEE IT IN YOU AND ADMIRE YOU FOR IT.

EXPECT THE BEST FROM YOURSELF AND GET IT!!

WHAT DO YOU CHOOSE TO DO WITH YOUR LIFE?

("Life's Similes")

CHOICES

A Delicate Balance in Sand Tones by Bernard Huff

An original sand painting created by Bernard Huff with selected colors of fine grains of sand.

Indianapolis Professional Association, Inc.
EDUCATION &
MENTORING
IPA
ECONOMIC
DEVELOPMENT
NETWORKING

WHAT DO YOU CHOOSE TO DO WITH YOUR LIFE?

("LIFE'S SIMILES")

BY: ATTY. BERNARD HUFF (REVISED 10/13)

WHAT DO YOU CHOOSE TO DO WITH YOUR LIFE?

Mold and shape it like fine sand in an alluring sandpainting
for others to see and want to have?

Plan it for many useful purposes like precious sand on a
a beautiful beach?

Or use it like loose sand in a minute or hourglass, which falls
shapelessly and automatically to the bottom of a container and
continues to repeat itself through action by an external force.

WHAT DO YOU INTEND TO DO WITH YOUR LIFE?

WHAT DO YOU CHOOSE TO DO WITH YOUR LIFE?

Cultivate it like a healthy seed planted in a well-kept garden
and allow it to develop into a hardy mature plant with lovely
blooms?

Or handle it like a wildflower in a dense forest, which
struggles to survive and sometimes withers, but it often

overshadowed by towering trees and other more adaptable vegetation.

WHAT DO YOU INTED TO DO WITH YOUR LIFE?

WHAT DO YOU CHOOSE TO DO WITH YOUR LIFE?

Take complete control of it now and never let go?

Continue to adjust and improve it from one life transition to the next in preparing yourself for a productive and worthwhile life? Or just let it go like the loose sand in a minute or hour glass or the wildflower in the dense forest.

WHAT DO YOU INTEND TO DO WITH YOUR LIFE?

WHAT CAN YOU DO WITH YOUR LIFE?

The answer is personal, introspective, obvious and without limitation.

You can do anything you want to do with it.

THE CHOICE IS LEFT TO YOU!

43

TAKING THE NEXT STEP(S): MAXIMIZE YOUR EFFORT

PERSEVERE

44

Indianapolis Professional Association, Inc.
CATION &
ING
IPA
ECONOMIC
DEVELOPMENT

TAKING THE NEXT STEP(S): MAXIMIZE YOUR EFFORT

Success or victory may be just one step ahead of you, but you may have given up too soon and deprived yourself of the benefit or result.

Take those extra steps, if needed.

Make that next move, if necessary.

Maximize your effort, and

Stay until the end.

DON'T GIVE UP TOO SOON!

Put forth enough time and effort to achieve your goal or to complete your meaningful tasks.

You will learn from your personal experiences.

You will become aware of your hidden strength, and

You will be proud of the result of your effort.

DON'T GIVE UP TOO SOON!

When you have to make important decisions in your life, take in account and do the following things.

Thoroughly consider your options.

Make sound choices and decide wisely.

Follow-through with your action plan and make changes when needed.

Forge ahead until you visualize and reach that shining light of success or achieve that result for which you have aimed.

DON'T GIVE UP TOO SOON!

Reflections of being so close or having almost made it may bring momentary consolation to you, but they will not make you a winner or successful in your personal life endeavors.

PERSEVERE! STAY TO THE END! DON'T GIVE UP!

HOW SHOULD I SEE AND BE ME: THEN, NOW AND TOMORROW

("Introspection")

SOUL-SEARCHING

HOW SHOULD I SEE AND BE ME:

THEN, NOW AND TOMORROW

("INTROSPECTION")

BY: ATTY. BERNARD HUFF 10/13

Do I have the sincerity and openness to take a look at myself to see where I came, where I am now, and what's in store for **ME** tomorrow?

With much mental fortitude, I realize that I have to first examine ME and value my self-worth.

Then, I can respond to the following personal inquiries:

Who am I? What is my purpose in life? What have I done to get myself to this place in my life? Am I happy and content to be where I am? What do I want to do in the future with my life?

Perhaps, a reflection of my wants and needs will help to disclose who I am and where I am headed. What must I do that is within my power to get myself eventually to a life of satisfaction and fulfillment? How much should I be concerned with trying to achieve this aim in that my wants and needs change from time-to-time.

If the answers to these personal inquiries about my current and future states are unknown or too difficult for **ME** to determine at this juncture, what can I do to get ME from Point A to Point B and then to Point C in my life?

I realize and accept the fact that my feelings must be considered to determine who I am.

But, how do I really feel about my family, friends, acquaintances, others who come into my life through various encounters and **ME**.

Do I love or like **ME** a lot, a little? Or do I possess an innate feeling of indifference?

Am I afraid to see and accept who I am or just don't care about this introspection?

Why have I not given any deep thought to who I am and who I want to be in the future until now?

Now that I have considered this introspection. What choices do I have and what can I do with respect to my life?

Should I let life take its own course, become a follower of my instincts and accept the flow of life wherever it will lead **ME**?

Or should I carefully pave the way for each major stage and turning point in my life with a clear vision and take positive planned action to obtain a desired result?

After all of my soul-searching and apprehension about this introspection of **ME**,

I now understand and accept my faults, my weaknesses as well as my strong points,

my past and current feelings about others and **ME** especially.

I can truly and honestly feel and say that I like how far I have come, where I am headed, and what I am becoming.

But, most importantly, I have begun to love **ME**.

PERSONAS

("DIFFERENT PERCEPTIONS")

FACADES

PERSONAS

("DIFFERENT PERCEPTIONS")

BY BERNARD HUFF 10/13

Oftentimes, we possess two faces in our relationships with and responses to others and to various situations. First, we react inwardly and then give an outward expression. Must we always think before we speak or react?

These two human personas may not be the same and each could have a different effect if the other one is utilized. Which one is real?

This duality of our thought and response may be a necessary human trait?

Should we always present our true feeling in our interpersonal relationships and in our responses to situations or must we modify it?

Human nature compels us to be tactful, kind and respectful in our relationships with others and in certain situations. Do our personas come into play automatically?

Should we use our will power to control and gauge what we think along with a façade?

A façade which we often use is an effective tool upon which we can rely.

But, are we being truthful to ourselves when we continually use a façade in mostly all of our interpersonal relationships?

A façade is effective when it is use with discretion and without causing any emotional or physical pain or harm.

Equally important are the two perceptions of how we see ourselves and what others actually think of us in our interpersonal relationships?

It is self-evident that in some instances these two perceptions may differ, and that it may be difficult or impossible to discern what others think of us.

We may not see ourselves as others visualize who they think we are and we could be left with a feeling of rejection or acceptance.

Another person's first impression may be one of love, admiration, jealousy, envy, negativity or wonderment and that impression but could be unfair and baseless and does not truly reflect who we are.

What can we do to control our inward feelings, our external expressions and others' perceptions about us?

We can develop a sense of positive thoughts about ourselves and others and discreetly utilize it in our interpersonal relationships.

We can empower ourselves to feel good about ourselves.

This should lessen the negative thinking about how we feel about ourselves and a positive outlook on our perception as to how others feel about us.

Sometimes in life, there are those special and defining moments and occasions where one's love, respect and/or other good emotional feelings closely coincides with those of another or other persons.

The occurrence of these mutual feelings of unity and oneness may vary from person to person.

When they do happen, they become happy thoughts, pleasant and cherished memories, and they should never be forgotten.

SELF-EMPOWERMENT

("BOOTSTRAPPING AND MORE...")

CONFIDENCE

Indianapolis Professional Association, Inc.
EDUCATION &
MENTORING
IPA
ONOMIC
LOPMENT
NETWO

SELF-EMPOWERMENT
("BOOTSTRAPPING AND MORE...")
BY: ATTY. BERNARD HUFF

Many of us want to be self-empowered, but fail to do so due to our lack of knowledge.

The impatient ones are not willing to give enough consideration, time and effort needed to achieve self-empowerment.

Others do not try at all because of their negative attitudes, convictions and fear of failure.

Self-empowerment is a powerful, desirable, self-engaging and driving force to have.

What must you have or acquire and what action should you take to empower yourself?

Self-empowerment requires knowledge, mental fortitude, determination, self-awareness and self-motivation or action.

Do you possess all of these qualities?

If so, lift yourself upward and onward from your present state?

If not, what can you do to acquire these attributes which you need for your personal upward mobility?

To be self-empowered, you must be aware of your strong points and weaknesses, and make improvements and adjustments to them as you move forward with your life.

Being self-empowered is more than standing on your own two feet.

It motivates you to move forward and take the necessary steps to sustain a productive and worthwhile life.

Self-empowerment requires preparation and a readiness to take on life challenges which face you today and tomorrow?

If you are now prepared, face and deal with them.

If you are not ready, prepare yourself!

You may not be able to pull yourself up by your "boot straps" alone. In your preparation, you may have to request and rely on the assistance of others and you should do so without any hesitation. Don't consider the help from others as a sign of personal weakness, but as a necessary tool for you to become self-empowered.

To achieve and retain self-empowerment, you must have self-control and staying power.

Inwardly, you must strive to remain mentally strong and stay in control of your emotions.

Outwardly, you must be aware of your relationships with others and male personal adjustments as needed in various situations and under different circumstances.

If you practice and adhere to these qualities, you can empower yourself and remained empowered.

EMPOWER YOURSELF! YOU CAN DO IT WITH YOUR KNOWLEDGE, STRENGTH, DETERMINATION, ENDURANCE AND SELF-CONTROL. EMPOWER YOURSELF! EMPOWER YOURSELF! EMPOWER YOURSELF! YOU CAN DO IT. YOU CAN DO IT. IT'S WITHIN YOU. EMPOWER YOURSELF! EMPOWER YOURSELF! EMPOWER YOURSELF! YOU CAN DO IT. YOU CAN DO IT. IT'S WITHIN YOU. EMPOWER YOURSELF! EMPOWER YOURSELF! EMPOWER YOURSELF! YOU WILL DO IT. YOU WILL DO IT! EMPOWER YOURSELF!

WE ARE
BETTER
THAN THIS!

A UNIFIED CRY FOR EQUALITY AND REFORMATION:

LET'S START NOW!

BY: ATTORNEY BERNARD HUFF

During a historic and significant time in 2020 and thereafter attributive and pertinent to the George Floyd's murder incident, there were diverse global, national, states and local outcries for social justice and racial equality. Leaders of the corporate business arena formed initiatives, made financial pledges and promised their companies' unbound support to combat systemic racism and bring forth equality for Blacks and other people of color. Specifically, with respect to this publicized court case, the Black Minnesota Attorney General in advance of the sentencing proposed a long prison term for the Defendant, Derek Chauvin due to his nine and a half minutes of suffocation of George Floyd which caused his death. In 2021, a diverse jury found the ex-police officer guilty on three felony counts. He was later sentenced to over twenty-two years' imprisonment.

As an aftermath, what can be done to obtain the most benefits from this unified call to action to eliminate racial injustices and obtain equality for all in America? How can this great nation be transformed into a living rainbow of citizenry with equal rights and privileges for everyone? Mentally, we can readily visualize that a unified movement with a determination for social justice and equality could achieve a greater human good. But, how can that unity be kept alive and continued with concerted action until the desired result is reached? In other words, how and where do we start to bring about a CHANGE?

From a local perspective, what can we do collectively and individually to change this city with a diverse populace into a safe living where equality for all people in every respect is an ongoing REALITY? Also, what will happen in the corporate arena after the George Floyd's case is no longer newsworthy? Will many of those corporate promises, initiatives and pledges along with the guilty verdicts become a passing sound and fury? Will most of the major corporate promises fade away without rectification? Also, will the promised corporate financial support and commitments become appeasements with no follow-through and/or material changes and noticeable improvements and the racial disparities continue to exist?

What can be done now and continued to counter appeasements and to encourage the corporate community to follow through with its promises, initiatives, pledges and resources to combat systemic racism and inequality? Through joint efforts by organizations and individuals, an effective strategy can be developed and appropriate action taken to address/combat racial disparities.

Also, monitoring may be needed to assure that corporate commitments are kept and become real and beneficial. Concurrently, the corporate community can provide funds, personnel and other needed resources to help improve the plight of minority businesses, organizations and individuals. Additionally, each concerned person can discuss and enlighten each other in a civil manner about racial and other minority issues of concern.

Social justice and equality for ALL, including people of color, are innate human and civil rights which should not be taken away or compromised. Are America and this city ready for everyone to have these human rights? Can the "AMERICAN DREAM" become a reality for ALL? If so, what should be done to make it happen? Specific federal, state and local resources are needed and should be utilized to eradicate existing disparities in communities of color and to improve specific areas such as education, economic development, youth and human services, criminal and civil justice reforms and other essential needs to bring about equality? How can these resources be obtained and utilized? From a national perspective, President Biden recently issued in early 2021 executive orders with broad coverage to combat and rectify systematic racial discrimination. It remains to be seen as to how these executive orders will be enforced and the results and improvement they will make.

What else can be done both by minority-led organizations and the corporate community? Business and individual leaders from both sectors can initiate joint forums to engage in dialogue to explore prevalent racial issues and propose solutions. Also, the business community should include within their operational plans, various support for minority organizations and groups with ample funds, personnel and other needed resources for them to strive. Lastly, for organizations and groups to obtain the greatest benefits and results from this current outcry for racial equality and injustice, they should develop and execute an action plan in line with their charitable mission and follow-through with it.

As U.S. citizens, African-Americans and other people of color who face systematic racism, disparities and injustices, what do we want and need? Answer: A changed humanity with equal rights and privileges for ALL. When should we start to make it happen? Answer: RIGHT NOW!

EFFECTIVE NETWORKING REVISITED

BY: BERNARD HUFF, ATTORNEY AT LAW/ MEDIATOR

The information imparted in this article on the commonly used term "NETWORKING" is viewed from the African-American author's perspective. It is based on his wide and diverse range of social and business experiences and contacts. Even though this information has universal application, some specific points were proposed and are directed to minority business persons and professionals in order to get them to learn how to network more effectively to achieve the greatest economic, social or charitable gain. Networking is more than just a mere social or business, social, charitable or have another motive. Too much lip service has been given to networking generally as a fashionable business and social term rather than to its use as a tool for getting business and clients or obtaining an economic or charitable gain. However, during this time of wide and current use of technology, effective networking can still be achieved.

Effective networking will work in almost any job, business, profession or social setting if one learns how to do it right. Networking has now become a perennial catchword. It is often used and misused with little or no thought being given to its meaning or without any defined purpose for its use. Oftentimes, it is casually mentioned in business and social conversations with no desire to generate business, promote a charitable purpose or to obtain an economic gain. Networking for the sake of networking often becomes a social, purposeless and non-beneficial activity. If it is done within a charitable organization on a wide scale basis, it may be a misuse of human and monetary resources.

What exactly is networking? How can African-Americans and other minorities network more effectively? First, effective networking is colorblind. One must have a clear vision of what it means and how to apply it to his or her specific situation, business or interest. The writer defines networking as follows: "Networking is a direct or indirect communication or interaction with, between or among persons, groups or organizations to seek, obtain and/or impart information and/or assistance for business, economic and business advantage. In fundraising activities, minority organizations must plan for and keep focus on their charitable purposes.

African-Americans and other minorities not only should become aware and take advantage of existing business and economic opportunities, they should create additional ways to effectively network within and without the minority community. It is necessary for their economic survivorship. The writer has witnessed that on several occasions in diverse settings during networking events, many African-Americans and other ethnic minorities have allowed someone else to be "in the driver's seat". They have been reluctant to "toot their own horns". In order to become and stay competitive, they must effectively convince others to buy their goods and services or support their organizational programs and other activities.

Effective networking is accomplished by practicing and perfecting one's skills in business and social settings and through electronic means (websites, emails, etc.). It doesn't develop automatically. Once perfected, it can have a broad appeal and bring about many benefits and successful results. Effective networking consists of (1) making an appropriate business or social connection; (2)

obtaining a follow-up lead to obtain a potential economic, social or charitable benefit; and (3) consummating a business or social relationship by getting a benefit. Business and social etiquette should be applied. Don't "prey" on persons who you know.

Also, one who wants to become skillful at networking sometimes may have to leave his/her comfort zone in order to develop a business or social relationship to obtain economic or charitable gain. Effective networking may involve reciprocity with respect to sharing of information and other resources with others. One may have to do business with someone in order to get business. Lastly, effective networking often requires a mutual knowledge of persons involved in the networking process. People normally do business with someone they know or have been referred to by someone else they know. In conclusion, networking has become an integral part of our business and social lives. It is essential that we learn how to do it effectively and with a purpose.

MAIN BENEFITS OF EFFECTIVE NETWORKING

1. Creates a personal awareness of the current market conditions for goods, services or charitable causes;

2. Adds more exposure to different and diverse, social and business relationships;

3. Generates sound leads and good referrals;

4. Is usually successful with sufficient follow-up efforts and quality contacts;

5. Could enhance the benefits to nonprofit organizations if their charitable purposes are put forth as their main focus points; and

6. Could add to the personal growth and generate more business or economic gain and favorable recognition in the business world for both individuals and organizations if networking is successful and is done in a professional and meaningful manner.

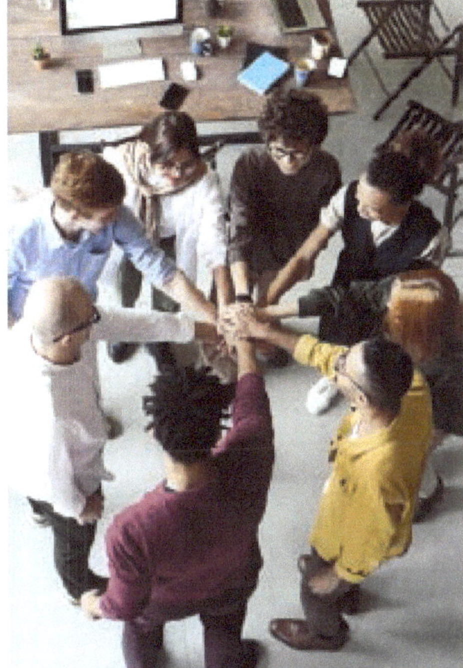

"DIVERSITY: THE AMERICAN WAY"
By: Bernard Huff, Attorney at Law

WHAT IS DIVERSITY? WHY DOES IT MATTER? HOW IS IT REALLY PRACTICED IN AMERICA? First, it's important to note that diversity comes into play where there is a significant number of persons of different races, national origin, various ethnic groups and sexes in a general population. But, it becomes problematic or doubtful whether real diversity can be achieved in certain settings where the total number of an affected group is limited, the requirements and/or qualifications are stringent and challenges are made. This is especially true with respect to the obtainment of diversity which requires direct and oftentimes multiple action to try or obtain a desired result. A positive result does not always come from action taken? In some instances, there are challenges made. In others, diversity efforts are terminated due to pressure and/or voluntary action.

Diversity may be a gradual process in which its progress and results are viewed infrequently. To monitor and measure its effects, the various settings, current status and the action taken should be viewed. If deficiencies are readily detected, what can and should be done to bring about improvements? In primary, secondary and higher education setting, how should diversity be achieved and practices with respect to student enrollment, teaching and administrative positions? What about training and upward mobility? In private industry, how may top administrative positions and corporate boards be diversified? In public employment – both locally and nationally – is there a real concern for diversity? Where and how is it being practiced?

In practice, who are the diversity recipients? Are women of color – Blacks and Hispanics – considered in the LEAD-IN dialogue for meaningful high corporate positions and on large corporate boards? In the entertainment industry, movies especially, are foreign born blacks being given more recognition than Black-American of slave ancestry. Who are the current recipients of diversity initiatives in both public and private higher educational institutions with respect to student enrollment?

How can the number and participation by blacks and Hispanics be significantly improved in meaningful jobs in high tech industry and in STEM initiatives? There are continuing openings in software development, design, product management, technical consulting and sales and marketing. The U.S. Bureau of Labor Statistics predicts that the hiring of software developers alone will grow 22% from 2012 to 2022 which is twice the average for all occupations. According to a Forbes 2013 survey, INDIANAPOLIS is among the cities which creates the most technology jobs. Companies here oftentimes struggle to find skilled workers. How can Blacks and Hispanics become a part of this growth? What specific training – collaborative and individual – can be initiated and successfully implemented to get a much higher and significant representation of these two minority groups? Lastly, what is the current state of DIVERSITY in your city or town?

The Brown Madonna (In Sand Tones) by Bernard Huff

Another fine sand painting with selected colors of sand created

by Bernard Huff.

M-A-M-A

(A HANDY MATERNAL ACRONYM FOR INDIVIDUAL, BUSINESS AND ORGANIZATIONAL USAGE AND GUIDANCE.)

Like a baby needs his/her mama to survive and grow, a nonprofit organization also needs a M-A-M-A in order to survive and continue to operate in an efficient, effective and legal manner to continue to perform its charitable missions. Please remember and apply the following coined acronym with a meaning and usage given to the single letters stated below to your nonprofit operation/programs.

M – MONEY: All nonprofit organizations should continually generate sufficient finds for its operation, administration and charitable programs. These funds routinely come from membership dues, fund-raising events, corporate sponsorships, grants and other solicitations. There should be proper in-house accountability for the receipt and expenditure of all funds regardless of their origin/source.

A – ADMINISTRATION: A nonprofit organization must have an effective administration. All officers should perform all of their duties; task force and committees should timely meet, report and successfully implement their programs and other activities. All Board Members should attend meetings, support and become actively involves in all of the nonprofit organization's major activities.

M – MEMBERS: Like money, the involvement of and the continuing recruitment of new members are two more lifebloods of nonprofit organizations. An effective recruitment mechanim should be put in place to obtain members with different expertise and training to help fulfill the charitable mission.

A – ATTENDANCE: The meetings, programs and events of a nonprofit organization must have sufficient attendance in order to be successful. In some cases, electronic advertisement alone is insufficient. Telephonic, word of mouth and other personal contacts are often needed to increase attendance.

PREPARED BY: ATTORNEY BERNARD HUFF

THAT'S WHAT M-A-M-A MEANS!